Abraham friend of God

Story by Penny Frank

Illustrated by Tony Morris

Presented to

Stuart Henderson

for

attendance

1988.

FAITH MISSION BOOKSHOP, 48 Upper Queen Street, Belfast

The Old Testament
tells the story of God's dealings with
his people-in good times and bad-and
his constant care for them.

God chose Abraham to be the
founder of the Hebrew nation-God's
'chosen people'.

'I will give you many descendants,'
God promised him, 'and they will
become a great nation.'

Abraham trusted God, and God kept
his promises.

Copyright © 1984 Lion Publishing

Published by
Lion Publishing plc
Icknield Way, Tring, Herts, England
ISBN 0 85648 729 5
Lion Publishing Corporation
10885 Textile Road, Belleville,
Michigan 48111, USA
ISBN 0 85648 729 5
Albatross Books
PO Box 320, Sutherland, NSW 2232, Australia
ISBN 0 86760 513 8

First edition 1984

All rights reserved

Printed and bound in Hong Kong
by Mandarin Offset International (HK) Ltd.

**British Library Cataloguing in
Publication Data**

Frank, Penny
 Abraham friend of God. – (The Lion
 Story Bible; 4)
 1. Abraham – Juvenile literature
 I. Title   II. Morris, Tony
 222'.110924   BS580.A3

 ISBN 0-85648-729-5

Abraham and his wife Sarah lived in
the town of Ur, in the land of Babylon.
One day God told him to leave his
home to go to a new land – a land
which God would give to Abraham and
his family.

Abraham and Sarah had no map. God
showed them the way. It was a long,
long journey and at night they put up a
big tent to sleep in. On and on they
travelled through many countries.

6

Abraham and Sarah were both old, but
still they had no children. God said to
them, 'Look at the grains of dust on the
path. Look at the stars above your tent
at night. One day your family will be as
many as that – too many to count.' And
still Abraham trusted God.

7

They were glad when they came to the new land. It had been such a long journey. There was no house to live in, so they lived in their big tent.

One day Abraham saw some men going by. 'Please come in and sit down', he said. 'We will get you something to eat.'

'That would be good,' said the men, 'because we have an important message for you. Your wife Sarah is going to have a baby boy.'

Sarah heard what they said and laughed. 'It is too late,' she said. 'We are too old now.'

God was sorry that Sarah did not
believe the men he had sent. But soon
Sarah knew that the message was true.
She was going to have a baby.

‘Perhaps nothing is too hard for God,’
she said.

When the baby boy was born, Abraham and Sarah were very happy. They called him Isaac. God had kept his promise.

God had given Abraham a new land
and he had given him a son. How
Abraham loved Isaac.

God loved Abraham. But he wanted to make sure that Abraham trusted him just as much as when he had first come to the new land.

So God said to Abraham, 'Take this son you love so much and go to the mountains you can see. I want you to offer him to me as a sacrifice.'

Poor Abraham! He wished there was
some other way to show God his love.
But he obeyed God. He took Isaac to the
mountains with some firewood and a
knife.

Isaac looked at the heap of stones on the mountain. He saw the knife and the wood.

'What shall we offer to God on the stones to show that we love him?' he asked.

Abraham was very sad but he told
Isaac that they must trust God to give
them something to put on the stones.

God did not want Isaac to die. He did not want Abraham and Sarah to be unhappy. He just wanted to be sure that Abraham would still trust and obey him.

Abraham put Isaac on top of the stones.
He picked up the knife to kill Isaac.

Then God called, 'Abraham, stop!
Look, I have given you the animal in
that bush behind you.'

God knew now that Abraham really did
trust him. He would obey whatever the
cost. Abraham and Isaac were so
happy. They thanked God as they made
the sacrifice.

They talked about what had happened as they went down the mountain. They were so glad that they could trust God.

And as God had promised, through Isaac and his children Abraham's family did become a great nation.

The Lion Story Bible is made up of 52 individual stories for young readers, building up an understanding of the Bible as one story – God's story – a story for all time and all people.

The Old Testament section (numbers 1-30) tells the story of a great nation – God's chosen people, the Israelites – and God's love and care for them through good times and bad. The stories are about people who knew and trusted God. From this nation came a Saviour, for all people everywhere, Jesus Christ.

Abraham, friend of God is a story about a promise. God promised Abraham that he would become the father of a great nation. It is also a story about faith – Abraham's trust in God.

The story of Abraham is told in the Old Testament book of Genesis, beginning at chapter 12.

In Abraham's day it was not unusual for people to offer up a child in sacrifice to their gods – to win favour. God was not like that. When he asked Abraham to sacrifice his only son, he was setting a test. He wanted to be sure that Abraham would trust him and do as he said, no matter what. Abraham passed the test! As a result God's people down the ages have looked up to him as a great man of faith.

In the next story, number 5: *Isaac finds a wife*, we see how God kept his promise to Abraham.